Original title:
Winter's Bright Serenity

Copyright © 2024 Swan Charm
All rights reserved.

Author: Johan Kirsipuu
ISBN HARDBACK: 978-9908-1-1369-2
ISBN PAPERBACK: 978-9908-1-1370-8
ISBN EBOOK: 978-9908-1-1371-5

Frosted Pinions of Elegance

In the glimmering light, the snowflakes dance,
Stars twinkle bright, in a festive trance.
Joyful laughter fills the starry night,
Hearts intertwine, in pure delight.

Tables adorned with treats so sweet,
Families gather, love's heartbeat.
Merry voices blend, a harmonious song,
Warming the chill, where we all belong.

Gifts wrapped in colors, shiny and bold,
Stories shared, as warmth unfolds.
Every moment cherished, memories align,
In this season of magic, hearts brightly shine.

Beneath the mistletoe, we share a smile,
Creating our magic, wrapping joy in style.
Frosted pinions whisper tales of grace,
In a festive embrace, we find our place.

Echoes of a Snowy Dawn

Whispers of winter dance in the light,
Snowflakes flutter, a joyful sight.
Children's laughter fills the air,
Joy in hearts, warmth everywhere.

Fires crackle, glowing bright,
Hands held close, a sweet delight.
Stories shared, dreams take flight,
Under stars, the world feels right.

A Canvas of Glowing White

Nature's brush paints purest white,
Blankets of snow in the calm twilight.
Sleds and laughter, a festive cheer,
Echoes of joy as loved ones draw near.

Footprints traced in frosty ground,
Magic of winter all around.
Hot cocoa served with marshmallow layers,
Warm embraces, sweet moments savored.

Celestial Reflections at Frost's Edge

Moonlight glistens on frozen streams,
Sparkling diamonds, woven dreams.
Night's embrace brings peace anew,
Stars twinkle as shadows accrue.

Frosty breath in the chilled air,
Whispers of wonder, moments rare.
Beneath the sky, our spirits soar,
Celebration echoes forevermore.

Ethereal Landscapes Under Moonbeams

Silvery glow on the sleeping pines,
Mystic nights where the world aligns.
Laughter mingles with frosty breath,
Chasing shadows, defying death.

Glistening paths where dreams collide,
Hearts united, love as our guide.
In the silence, joy does abound,
Marching forth, our hopes unbound.

Serenity in the Silent Night

The moon hangs low, a silver glow,
Whispers of peace in the frosty air.
Footprints dance in the blanket of snow,
Joyful laughter mingles everywhere.

Candles flicker in warm embrace,
Hearts aglow in the chilly night.
Each moment savored, a gentle grace,
Under the stars, the spirits take flight.

Families gather, stories unfold,
Shared memories wrapped in delight.
In this silent night, love's being told,
A tapestry woven, so pure and bright.

Dappled Light and Frosty Air

The sun peeks through the frosted trees,
Casting shadows of fleeting gold.
Children giggle in the winter freeze,
Their rosy cheeks a joy to behold.

Glistening paths of shimmering white,
Echoes of footsteps, a cheerful sound.
Festive spirits take wondrous flight,
In a frosty realm where joy is found.

Hot cocoa brews, a sweet delight,
Marshmallows dance on the warm surface.
Embracing the warmth on a cold, clear night,
We wrap our hearts in this cherished place.

A Spectacle of Stars and Ice

Above, a canvas of sparkling light,
The universe twinkles in festive display.
Icicles hang like diamonds bright,
Nature's jewels in a playful array.

Snowflakes tumble in graceful delight,
Each one unique, a delicate laugh.
We gather together, hearts feeling right,
Sharing dreams as we warm by the hearth.

Outdoors the world wears a crystalline crown,
While cheerful songs float through the air.
In this spectacle, cares feel drowned,
We revel in joy, free from despair.

Illumination in the Frost

The streets aglow with warm, soft light,
Lanterns sway in the cool evening breeze.
Families gather, a heartwarming sight,
Their laughter dancing among the trees.

Wreaths of greenery, ribbons so bright,
Adorning the houses, all spirits lifted.
In every window, a joyous invite,
As the spirit of giving is lovingly gifted.

Chill in the air, but warmth in our hearts,
With every carol, our souls intertwine.
A festive cheer that never departs,
In this magical moment, together we shine.

Starry Nights and Snowy Dreams

Under a sky of twinkling light,
Snowflakes dance in pure delight.
Joyful laughter fills the air,
As friends gather everywhere.

Candles flicker with a glow,
Whispers of love in the snow.
Warmth of hearts, a festive cheer,
Magic lingers, year after year.

Trees adorned with shining hue,
Brightly lit, all draped in blue.
Beneath the stars, dreams take flight,
Embracing the bliss of the night.

Carols sung with merry glee,
Echoes of joy, wild and free.
In this season, spirits soar,
Starry nights, we all adore.

Nature's Breath in the Chill

Gentle winds through branches weave,
Nature whispers, all believe.
Frosty patterns dress the trees,
Creating beauty on the breeze.

Crisp and bright, the mornings gleam,
Sunshine dances, warm with dream.
Footprints crunch on snowy trails,
Holiday spirit never fails.

Laughing children, sleds in tow,
Joy and wonder all aglow.
Glistening hills invite the fun,
Chasing shadows in the sun.

With each breath, a cloud of white,
Nature's pause in winter's light.
In this moment, hearts are kind,
Chill and warmth, beautifully entwined.

Glowing Embers Against the Dark

In the hearth, the embers glow,
Casting warmth in night's shadow.
Gathered close, stories unfold,
Laughter shared, the fire bold.

Stars above in velvet skies,
Twinkling softly, merry sighs.
The chill outside starts to fade,
By the light, memories made.

With every cheer, our spirits rise,
Beneath the cosmos' vast surprise.
Festive hearts, together we stand,
Creating magic, hand in hand.

As the night wraps round us tight,
We celebrate love's pure light.
Glowing embers sing their song,
In this moment, we belong.

Soft Lullabies of the Cold

Snowflakes whisper to the ground,
In their grace, a peace is found.
Under blankets, cozy tight,
We find warmth in winter's night.

The world outside, a perfect scene,
Frosty windows, all serene.
Gentle lullabies in air,
Nature's hush, a soothing prayer.

Hot cocoa with marshmallows sweet,
Fireside chats, a chance to meet.
Sharing dreams as twilight falls,
Winter's charm, its magic calls.

With every heartbeat, love is near,
Season of joy, good cheer premiere.
Soft lullabies of winter's hold,
Wrap us gently, brave and bold.

The Silent Glow of Ice

In winter's hush, the starlight gleams,
Soft whispers dance in silver beams.
The frosty air, a blanket light,
Beneath the moon, our hearts take flight.

Each flake that falls, a gem, a wish,
In crystal coats, the world we kiss.
With laughter shared, the night unfolds,
In icy realms, our joy retold.

The trees are wrapped in shimm'ring white,
Their branches sway, a gentle sight.
We gather close, with spirits bright,
In winter's glow, hearts dance tonight.

Prismatic Snowflakes on Gray

Upon a canvas, gray and low,
Dance all the flakes, a vibrant show.
Each catches light, a rainbow's hue,
Transforming scenes, a magic view.

Children's laughter fills the air,
With every snowball, joy we share.
The world becomes a wonderland,
As prismatic dreams lie soft and grand.

We bundle up, in warmth we thrive,
Together, feeling so alive.
Embrace the cold, let spirits soar,
In every flake, we yearn for more.

Starry Nights and Crystal Fields

Beneath the sky, so vast and clear,
The starry night draws us near.
With crystal fields that sparkle bright,
We walk in silence, hearts alight.

Whispers of wind, a gentle grace,
As moonlight paints each frosty space.
In awe we stand, beneath the glow,
In dreams of wonder, feelings flow.

A symphony of night unfolds,
With stories whispered, yet untold.
In harmony, our spirits climb,
Together, lost in frosted time.

Reflections of Calm in Chill

In quiet corners, stillness reigns,
As winter's touch embraces planes.
Reflections dance on frozen lakes,
A canvas vast, where magic wakes.

The air is crisp, the world feels new,
In chilly moments, dreams break through.
With every breath, the calm we seek,
In snowy fields, our hearts will speak.

We gather close, a cozy band,
With mugs of warmth in every hand.
Reflecting peace, we feel the thrill,
In moments bright, against the chill.

The Challenged Warmth of Daylight

The sun peeks through the clouds, bright and bold,
A dance of shadows, stories unfold.
Children laugh, their joy runs free,
In every corner, pure glee we see.

Balloons float high in the azure sky,
Voices blend as the moments fly.
Picnics spread on lush green grass,
The warmth of love in every pass.

Golden rays embrace the day,
As laughter echoes, come what may.
Friendships bloom like flowers in spring,
Togetherness is the sweetest thing.

As twilight whispers, a promise to stay,
The night unveils a magical play.
With hearts aglow and spirits bright,
We celebrate this wondrous sight.

Snow Covered Serenity

The world transformed in blankets white,
Each flake a whisper of pure delight.
Children giggle in a playful race,
Snowmen stand guard, a frosty embrace.

Trees adorned with glistening light,
Twinkling stars in the chilly night.
From every window, warmth spills out,
Laughter and love are what it's about.

Cocoa warms hands, sweet and rich,
Stories are shared without a hitch.
Time slows down in this soft glow,
In snow covered serenity, spirits grow.

As moonlight dances on the snow,
Dreams take flight, and joy we sow.
With every snowfall, a fresh canvas laid,
Memories made that will never fade.

Shivering Silhouettes in Twilight

In the soft hush of fading light,
Shadows stretch, bidding day goodnight.
Laughter dances in the cooling breeze,
Whispers of warmth among the trees.

Lanterns flicker, casting a glow,
Footsteps crunch on the frosty snow.
Amidst the chill, hearts find cheer,
In shivering silhouettes, we draw near.

Firelight crackles, tales are spun,
Beneath the stars, we feel the fun.
Hot apple cider, sweet, divine,
Moments shared, hearts entwined.

As twilight deepens its gentle reign,
We gather close, forget the strain.
In the night's embrace, we hold tight,
Together we shine, in festive delight.

A Moment in Silvery Glow

Beneath the moon's soft, silvery hue,
Radiance dances, a dream come true.
Laughter echoes in the tranquil night,
Magic swirls in the gentle light.

Stars twinkle high, a canvas of dreams,
In the cool air, joy softly beams.
Life's simple treasures tucked in a song,
In this moment, we all belong.

Warmth in our hearts, friendship aglow,
United we stand, in this sacred show.
The world fades away, just you and me,
Lost in the sparkle of serendipity.

As shadows fade into memory's fold,
The beauty of now is ours to hold.
In a moment so pure, we dance and sway,
In the silvery glow, we choose to stay.

Silent Gleam of Frost

In the stillness of the night,
A blanket soft and white,
Twinkling lights like stars above,
Whispers of the season's love.

Joyful laughter fills the air,
Magic weaves without a care,
Gentle glow from candles bright,
Hearts are warm, spirits light.

Footsteps crunch in sparkling snow,
As the merry moments flow,
Children's faces full of cheer,
In this festive time of year.

Wrapped in dreams, we raise a toast,
To the ones we love the most,
Each smile a cherished gift we find,
In this frost, our hearts aligned.

Crystal Whisper on a Frosted Morning

Beneath a sky of crystal blue,
The world awakens fresh and new,
Each branch adorned with icy lace,
Nature's beauty, a soft embrace.

Frosted grass in sunlight glows,
A sparkling dance as day bestows,
Chirping birds bring sweet delight,
In the warmth of morning light.

Children bundled, laughter rings,
Building dreams on snowflakes' wings,
Every face aglow with cheer,
Joyous moments held so dear.

As the air brims with delight,
We gather close, hearts shining bright,
In the hush of winter's charm,
Feel the love and hold it warm.

The Stillness of Snow-Kissed Dreams

In the quiet, dreams unfold,
Stories from the young and old,
Snowflakes dance with gentle grace,
A magical and wondrous place.

Fires crackle, shadows play,
Memories woven in the gray,
Warmth of smiles around the hearth,
In this season of our birth.

Underneath the twinkling lights,
We gather close on snowy nights,
Friendship glows like lantern beams,
In the stillness of our dreams.

Laughter lingers on the breeze,
Wishes carried through the trees,
A tapestry of love we weave,
In this quiet, we believe.

Where Stars Dance on Chilled Air

Above us twinkle, stars align,
Casting wishes, bright and fine,
In the chill, we find our song,
Together, where we all belong.

Frosty breath in the night sky,
Echoes of our laughter high,
As we twirl and spin with glee,
In this moment, wild and free.

Candles flicker, shadows sway,
Guiding us through the festive play,
Every heartbeat echoes cheer,
In this magic, we are near.

So raise a glass to joy's embrace,
With every smile, we find our place,
In the dance of stars so bright,
We celebrate this wondrous night.

The Heartbeat of Nature in Snowy Silence

In the hush of falling snow,
Whispers dance with gentle grace.
Branches dressed in frosty glow,
Nature's calm, a warm embrace.

Footprints trace a story sweet,
Children laugh, their faces bright.
In this world, our hearts will meet,
Frozen moments, pure delight.

Stars peek through the velvet night,
Twinkling softly, shining bold.
Winter's breath, a soft invite,
Tales of wonder to be told.

By the fire, stories flow,
Cocoa warms our hearts anew.
In the silence, love will grow,
Heartbeat strong, like morning dew.

Glistening Silence of the Sleeping Earth

Snowflakes twirl in silent flight,
Kissing earth with tender care.
Blankets white, a pure delight,
Nature rests, without a care.

Evergreens in frosted lace,
Guardians of the glistening light.
Each branch a memory, a place,
Holding dreams of winter's night.

Moonbeams shimmer on the ground,
Magic lingers in the air.
In this silence, joy is found,
A promise of a love to share.

Candles flicker, shadows play,
Gathered close, we sing and cheer.
In this moment, hearts will sway,
To the melody we hold dear.

Tranquil Dreams on Icy Tides

Waves of whispers softly sing,
Icy shores in twilight glow.
Dreams take flight on winter's wing,
Gentle tides begin to flow.

Underneath the silver haze,
Peaceful moments dance and glide.
Frosted dreams of bright, warm days,
In this stillness, hearts reside.

Ocean's lull, a soothing sound,
Guiding us to shores of peace.
In this place, we are unbound,
Finding joy that will not cease.

Stars above twinkle and gleam,
As the night wraps us in care.
In our minds, we softly dream,
Of adventures we will share.

A Symphony of Icicles in the Sunlight

Icicles hang with glistening grace,
Tinkling softly, nature's chime.
In the sun, they shine and trace,
A melody that beats in time.

Laughter bubbles in the breeze,
Children building snowmen grand.
Joy erupts with playful ease,
A festive spirit shared by hand.

Hot cocoa steaming, spirits lift,
Bundled close, we share a smile.
Every moment feels a gift,
In this warmth, we pause awhile.

As evening falls, the stars align,
Lighting up our winter nights.
Festive hearts in sweet design,
Together, we embrace the lights.

Serenity in Silver and Blue

The night sky glimmers bright,
Silver stars dance in the blue.
Laughter echoes through the air,
Joyful hearts are all around.

Candles flicker, soft and warm,
Whispers carry gentle tunes.
Families gather close tonight,
In this festive, peaceful glow.

The moonlight casts a lovely hue,
Reflecting off the snowy ground.
Children's eyes shine with delight,
As dreams of wonder come alive.

In every corner, love does bloom,
Underneath the stars' soft gaze.
Serenity wraps like a shawl,
Embracing all in silver blue.

The Quiet Embrace of Chill

Whispers of frost fill the air,
Nature dons her crystal dress.
The world slows down in sweet repose,
Wrapped in winter's gentle hush.

Footsteps crunch on frozen dew,
Every breath creates a cloud.
In the stillness, laughter rings,
As joy ignites the quiet night.

Under the glow of fairy lights,
Hearts beat in a joyful trance.
With every hug, warmth ignites,
In this festive, cherished dance.

The chill invites us to draw near,
To share in moments pure and bright.
Together we bask in the glow,
Of love that shines through all the night.

Illuminated Frost Patterns

Frosty lace upon the glass,
Artistry from winter's hand.
Nature's beauty, etched in white,
A tapestry, both pure and grand.

With every breath, we see the spark,
As light refracts on icy panes.
Children gaze in awe and wonder,
Delighted by the winter's gains.

Underneath the moon's soft glow,
Magic dances in the air.
In this festive, shimmering world,
Peace and joy are everywhere.

Frosty whispers tell a tale,
Of nights filled with love and cheer.
In every twinkle, every beam,
The spirit of the season's here.

Fresh Tracks in the Snow

New footprints mark the silent paths,
As laughter fills the winter air.
With every step, a story tells,
Of friendships cherished, beyond compare.

Children race to build a fort,
Snowballs fly from tiny hands.
Joy erupts like winter's sun,
Lighting up this frosty land.

Hot cocoa warms our chilly hands,
As we gather, hearts aglow.
In the warmth of shared delight,
We celebrate the fresh, white snow.

Each fresh track leads to joy anew,
A journey wrapped in laughter's cheer.
Together we create the magic,
In the wonder of winter here.

Frost's Embrace on the Earth

The morning light begins to play,
With sparkles bright in every way.
A silver blanket, soft and new,
Covers the world, a frosty hue.

Joyful laughter fills the air,
As children dance without a care.
Snowflakes swirl, a wondrous sight,
In the embrace of winter's light.

Each breath a cloud, so crisp and clear,
We gather close, our hearts sincere.
With love and warmth, we share this space,
In frost's embrace, we find our grace.

So raise a toast to chilly days,
With cheer that sparkles in the rays.
In winter's grasp, we'll celebrate,
Frost's gentle touch, oh how it's great.

Frosty Reflections in Still Water

Beneath the ice, the waters gleam,
Reflecting all like a waking dream.
A world transformed by winter's kiss,
In nature's arms, we find our bliss.

The trees stand tall, their branches bare,
As daylight dances without a care.
Crisp air whispers secrets of old,
In frosty reflections, stories unfold.

The laughter rolls across the lake,
In joyous hearts, our spirits wake.
We wander, wrapped in soft delight,
Where frosty magic sparks the night.

With every step, the world awakes,
As laughter rings, and silence breaks.
In still water's gleam, we find our song,
Frosty reflections, where we belong.

The Magic of Silent Alea

In silent alea, dreams take flight,
Beneath the stars, a scene so bright.
The world is hushed, as moments sway,
In twilight's glow, we drift away.

Laughter echoes through the night,
As joy ignites in every light.
With friends beside, we share a toast,
In the magic of moments, we find the most.

Softly the snowflakes kiss our cheeks,
Woven tales within the peaks.
Together, hearts entwined in cheer,
The magic of alea draws us near.

So let us dance 'neath the silver sky,
With frosty wings, we laugh and fly.
In silent alea, our spirits blend,
A festive night, where dreams transcend.

Glinting Light on Frozen Waters

Upon the lake, a shimmer glows,
Where glinting light in winter flows.
Each ripple sings a frosty tune,
As laughter sparkles beneath the moon.

In icy realms, we skate with glee,
A wondrous dance, just you and me.
With every swirl, our joy ignites,
In frozen waters, magic lights.

The world aglow, a canvas bare,
We paint our dreams in chilly air.
Hand in hand, we chase delight,
Through glinting light, our hearts take flight.

So gather close, let's share our cheer,
In winter's grasp, love draws us near.
With frozen waters, let's take a chance,
In glinting light, let's join the dance.

The Night's Gentle Embrace

Under the stars, laughter spills,
Joyful echoes dance on the hills.
Candles flicker with warm, soft light,
We gather close, hearts feeling bright.

The moon hangs low, a silver pearl,
In its glow, our dreams unfurl.
Voices blend in sweet refrain,
Every moment like gentle rain.

Glowing faces, smiles abound,
In this embrace, love's magic found.
Stories shared of days long past,
In this serenity, our souls are cast.

As the night wraps us in delight,
With every heartbeat, pure and bright.
Memories forged, together we spin,
In the night's embrace, we all win.

Shimmering Fields in Solitude

In the quiet, where the breezes sigh,
Glistening fields stretch wide and high.
Stars above, like diamonds they gleam,
In this solitude, we softly dream.

Whispers of grass and crickets' play,
Nature's orchestra leads the way.
Moonlit paths where secrets hide,
In shimmering fields, we stroll with pride.

A tapestry woven, silent yet loud,
Under the cosmos, we feel so proud.
Footsteps mark our fleeting trails,
In this vastness, love never fails.

The night enfolds us in its grace,
With every heartbeat, we find our place.
In solitude together, we find our peace,
In shimmering fields, our worries cease.

Hushed Harmony of the Night

A lullaby sung by the trees,
The night is calm, a gentle breeze.
Stars align in the velvet sky,
In hushed harmony, we sigh.

Under the canopy, shadows play,
Whispers echo, gently sway.
Moments linger, sweet and rare,
In this silence, we breathe the air.

Fireflies wink in twilight's glow,
Each one dancing, putting on a show.
With hearts united, we find our song,
In this harmony, we all belong.

The night unfolds, its magic vast,
In shared embrace, the moments last.
Together we dwell, in peace we find,
In this hushed harmony, soul and mind.

Frosted Memories of the Heart

In winter's breath, the world a dream,
Blanketed soft with a sparkling gleam.
Frosted air wraps around our souls,
In shared warmth, the heart consoles.

Childhood laughter dances in the snow,
Muffled whispers where the chill winds blow.
Footprints traced in silvery white,
Carrying joy into the night.

Each flake a memory, fragile yet bright,
Woven together in the soft moonlight.
With every breath, we savor the past,
In frosted moments, we find peace at last.

Gathered close, our stories flow,
In every heartbeat, the love will grow.
Through frost and chill, we shine like art,
Embraced forever, memories of the heart.

The Dance of Light on Winter's Edge

Twinkling lights hang from every tree,
Colors burst, wild and free.
Laughter rings through the crisp night,
As hearts ignite with pure delight.

Snowflakes twirl in a joyful spree,
Each one a gift, a mystery.
Footsteps crunch on the glittered snow,
Where warmth and merriment surely flow.

Gather near, let the stories unfold,
Of treasures past and dreams of gold.
With each embrace, a spark ignites,
In this dance of the winter lights.

Hands held tight, as the music plays,
Underneath the moon's soft rays.
Let the spirit of joy take flight,
In the dance of light on winter's edge.

Frosty Hues Beneath the Gentle Sun

Frosty hues paint the world bright,
Beneath the sun's soft, warm light.
Nature glimmers, a magical sight,
As smiles emerge, pure and light.

Children laugh, their cheeks aglow,
Building dreams in the crumbled snow.
Each snowman stands tall and proud,
Among a gathering of friends, so loud.

Sip hot cocoa, sweet and sweet,
In this cozy winter retreat.
The sun sets low, casting gold,
As tales of wonder drift and unfold.

Let's treasure these moments divine,
In frosty hues, where hearts intertwine.
Together we bask in joy's embrace,
Beneath the gentle sun's warm grace.

Luminescence Among Frostbitten Boughs

Stars twinkle on frostbitten boughs,
Nature whispers with solemn vows.
Each sparkle a story, a glimmer of night,
A festival of dreams, glowing bright.

The chill air dances with melodies sweet,
Footsteps echo in rhythmic beat.
Gathered close, the firelight's glow,
Spreads warmth in the silence, a comforting flow.

Hot drinks steaming, we share our cheer,
Under the blanket of winter near.
With every laugh, and every glance,
In this moment, we take a chance.

Together we sway, as the evening flows,
Enchanted by magic that winter bestows.
In luminescence, our spirits rise,
Among frostbitten boughs, beneath starry skies.

Whispers of Calm in the Frigid Air

In the frigid air, whispers soar,
Of joy and peace, hearts long for more.
Under blankets of soft, white snow,
We gather, sharing warmth as we glow.

The moon hangs low, casting gentle beams,
Awakening the world in tranquil dreams.
Candles flicker with a dance of light,
Shimmering softly through the starry night.

With laughter's echo, the night unfolds,
Every secret, every story told.
The fire crackles, spirits ignite,
In this calmness, everything feels right.

Let the winter's embrace wrap us tight,
As we cherish each moment, pure delight.
In whispers of calm, our hearts align,
In the frigid air, love's warmth will shine.

The Whisper of Snow-filled Nights

Snowflakes fall, like whispers soft,
Blankets of white drift gently aloft.
Children laugh, in joy they play,
As the moon sets the scene for a magical display.

Candles flicker in windows bright,
Warmth and comfort, a cozy sight.
The world wrapped in a silvery glow,
Hearts are lighter, as the festivities flow.

Mugs of cocoa, smiles abound,
Joyful echoes are all around.
Moments cherished, memories made,
In the magic of night, love won't fade.

So let us celebrate, hand in hand,
Under the stars in this winter land.
With laughter and cheer, we'll share the delight,
In the whisper of snow-filled nights.

A Reverie in Chill Colors

Winter's palette, a canvas grand,
Crimson berries, nature's hand.
Frosted branches, sparkles gleam,
In every corner, a joyful dream.

Scarves wrapped tight, we dance and sing,
In the air, jubilation we bring.
Footprints trace stories on fresh-fallen snow,
Through laughter and warmth, our spirits grow.

Fireplaces crackle, warmth ignites,
Gathered together on chilly nights.
The flicker of lights twinkles with glee,
In this reverie, we are wild and free.

So raise a toast to cold, bright days,
With love and joy, we lift our praise.
In every heart, a spark we find,
A reverie in chill colors, intertwined.

Celestial Flurries and Calm

Stars above in the velvet sky,
Winter's breath, a gentle sigh.
Celestial flurries, drifting slow,
A dance of light, a tranquil show.

Twinkling lights in the frosty air,
Shared laughter, moments rare.
We gather close, with warmth to share,
In every heartbeat, a love laid bare.

Snowmen stand, with snowy grins,
These simple joys, where warmth begins.
Hot spiced cider, the taste of cheer,
In the hush of night, our souls draw near.

As soft snowflakes kiss the ground,
In this calm, pure joy is found.
Celestial flurries, a wonderland night,
Under the moon, everything feels right.

The Quiet Dance of Icy Winds

Icy winds whisper through the trees,
As chilly air stirs with gentle ease.
Every breath a crystal sigh,
In this moment, time slips by.

Frosty branches sway in tune,
Under the gaze of a silver moon.
Children gather, eyes alight,
In the quiet dance of the snowy night.

Laughter mingles with the breeze,
Joyful hearts, gathering ease.
Snowflakes twirl, a waltz so grand,
We find our rhythm, hand in hand.

So as the winter wraps its arms tight,
We'll dance together, hearts alight.
In the splendor of this frosty dream,
The quiet dance of icy winds, supreme.

Glimmers on the Ice

Sparkling jewels in winter's dance,
Shimmering light in a frosty glance.
Children laughing, spirits soar,
Every moment, we adore.

Skaters glide with grace and ease,
Wind whispers through the swaying trees.
Hot cocoa warms our frozen hands,
Joyful times on glittering strands.

Candles flicker in the chilly night,
Fires crackle, hearts feel light.
Glimpses of magic fill the air,
A festive spirit everywhere.

As the stars begin to twinkle bright,
We gather close, hearts feeling right.
In this wonderland, we embrace,
Glimmers on the ice, a warm place.

Radiant Twilight Glow

Sunset hues paint the winter sky,
Laughter echoes, time slips by.
Twinkling lights on every street,
Warm embraces, moments sweet.

Children's joy in each small game,
Running wild, calling your name.
Snowflakes dance on the evening breeze,
Enchanting whispers among the trees.

Hot pies baking, scents fill the air,
Joyful faces everywhere.
Underneath the twilight's spell,
Stories shared, so much to tell.

Stars awaken, shining bright,
In this cozy, festive night.
Radiant glow, our hearts aglow,
Together in the warmth we know.

Chasing the Frosted Light

Amidst the flakes that softly fall,
We find delight, we feel it all.
Footprints left in purest snow,
Chasing the light, we laugh and glow.

Snowmen rise with carrot noses,
Childish laughter brightly poses.
Sleds and laughter fill the hill,
In this wonder, hearts are still.

Beneath the glow of the moon's embrace,
We twirl and spin in a joyful race.
With every shout, our voices blend,
In this magic, we'll never end.

As evening falls, we gather 'round,
With stories shared and peace found.
Chasing frost and joy's delight,
In the warmth of the chilly night.

Snowbound Tranquility

Softly blankets cover the ground,
In silence, beauty can be found.
Whispers of winter fill the air,
In snowbound peace, we rest and stare.

Branches bow with heavy grace,
Each flake a pure, unique embrace.
Children's laughter pierces the hush,
In this wonderland, we rush.

Icicles glisten in soft moonlight,
A tranquil world, so calm and bright.
Hot drinks steaming, fires aglow,
In every heart, a warmth will grow.

Gathered close, we share this night,
In the snow's embrace, pure delight.
Snowbound tranquility feels so right,
Together, we bask in festive light.

Twilight Glows Beneath the Frosty Veil

Twilight dances in colors bright,
Stars emerge, igniting the night.
Snowflakes twirl in a merry parade,
Nature's beauty will never fade.

Candles flicker, casting warm light,
Laughter echoes, hearts feel so right.
Footprints trace paths in the snow,
Joy abounds, let the good times flow.

Friends gather round, spirits align,
Sipping cocoa, tasting the divine.
Wishes whispered, hopes take flight,
Under the glow, all feels so bright.

As the moon smiles from above,
We celebrate the warmth of love.
In this festive, charming scene,
Life feels sweet, as if a dream.

A Canvas Painted with Icy Hues

A canvas spread by winter's hand,
Blankets of snow across the land.
Frosty breath hangs in the air,
Nature's art, a beauty rare.

Children giggle, making a mess,
Building snowmen in warm red dress.
The world shimmers in silver delight,
Painted edges in the soft moonlight.

Carols linger like gentle whispers,
Singing joy that gently glistens.
Every heart beats in time,
With laughter and love, pure as a rhyme.

Ice crystals dance, catching the eye,
Underneath the darkening sky.
Joy is woven into the scene,
A masterpiece, fresh and serene.

The Breath of Nature in a Colder Realm

The breath of nature, crisp and clear,
In every corner, festive cheer.
Trees adorned in sparkling frost,
In this season, we find no lost.

Warm embraces from friends so dear,
Creating memories to hold near.
Laughter rings through the frozen air,
In this moment, love is rare.

Candies and treats in colors bright,
Bring delight on a cold winter's night.
Songs of joy fill the evening skies,
As we gaze at the stars that rise.

Fireflies of joy, twinkling around,
In this colder realm, warmth is found.
With each breath, a promise we share,
In festive spirits, we show we care.

Echoes of Joy in a Snowbound Silence

In the snowbound silence, voices rise,
Echoes of joy beneath bright skies.
Every twinkle, every delight,
Warming hearts on this magical night.

Glistening paths where children play,
Creating memories that never fray.
Hot cocoa sipped by the crackling fire,
In the company of friends we admire.

Each snowfall whispers tales to unfold,
Of laughter shared and stories told.
Bells ringing, making spirits soar,
In this season, we long for more.

Joyful moments laid like a quilt,
In our hearts, the warmth is built.
Embraced by nature's frosty kiss,
We celebrate in sheer bliss.

Ghosts of Trees In a Shimmering White

Whispers dance on frosty air,
Branches glisten, tales to share.
Snowflakes twirl in joyous flight,
Embracing ghosts in shimmering white.

Laughter echoes through the glade,
Ancient spirits, unafraid.
With every flake, they spin and sway,
In this festive, winter ballet.

A hush surrounds the sleeping woods,
Colorful dreams, the heart alludes.
In twinkling light, their shadows play,
In the magic of a snow-kissed day.

Awakening the night's delight,
Glimmers spark beneath the light.
In wintry silence, joy ignites,
Ghosts of trees in dazzling sights.

Glimmering Stillness of the Chilled Horizon

Across the fields, a stillness falls,
Chilled horizons, nature calls.
Stars appear with a twinkling grin,
Festive whispers draw us in.

The moon like silver in the skies,
Enchanting dreams that never die.
Frosty breath of night does weave,
Magic moments we believe.

Glistening branches, shadows cast,
Embracing warmth that holds steadfast.
In the quiet, hearts unite,
Celebrating love's gentle light.

With every twinkle, the world aglow,
In the stillness, we all know.
Together we dance, hands in hand,
On this chilled and glimmering land.

The Magic of Midwinter's Embrace

In midwinter's frosty embrace,
Laughter echoes in this place.
Snowflakes shimmer like falling stars,
We gather close, forgetting scars.

Bonfires crackle, warmth ignites,
As we sing of joy-filled nights.
With every heart that joins the song,
In this magic, we all belong.

Candles flicker in gentle glow,
Creating paths where love can flow.
In the chilly air, we find our peace,
As winter's grip begins to cease.

Together we'll weave this tapestry,
Of memories bright, wild, and free.
In midwinter's magic, we embrace,
The warmth of home, a sacred space.

Celestial Lights Over Frosty Fields

Celestial lights dance in the night,
Painting frost with shimmering light.
Over fields, a heavenly glow,
Guiding all who wander slow.

Golden hues against the white,
Twinkling like stars, pure delight.
Joyful laughter fills the air,
A festive spirit everywhere.

In the stillness, hearts align,
Beneath the vast and endless shine.
Each moment shared, an endless gift,
In the warmth, our spirits lift.

Frosty fields, a canvas wide,
Under stars, we walk with pride.
Celestial lights, forever bright,
Guide us through this winter night.

A Palette of Silence in Crystal Patterns

In the hush of twilight's glow,
Colors blend, soft and slow.
Whispers of calm wrap the town,
As night drapes a silken gown.

Sparkling lights twinkle bright,
Reflecting dreams in the night.
Laughter floats through the air,
Joyful hearts find warmth to share.

Snowflakes glide like gentle sighs,
Underneath these vast, starry skies.
Each breath of winter tells a tale,
Of love and hopes that never pale.

Together we dance in delight,
In this festive, enchanting night.
With every step, happiness grows,
In a world that glitters and glows.

Hallowed Ground Under a Glistening Sky

Beneath the stars, spirits play,
Gathered close in warm array.
Voices rise like a sweet refrain,
Joyful hearts, with love unchained.

Candles light the tranquil scene,
Luminous, soft, and serene.
Stories shared by glowing fire,
Ignite in us a deep desire.

Snowflakes whisper their soft song,
In this moment, we belong.
The world outside fades away,
As we embrace the festive sway.

United under a starlit beam,
Life's a lovely, shared dream.
On this hallowed ground, we stand,
With joy and laughter, hand in hand.

Silent Snowflakes Dance

Silent snowflakes twirl and glide,
Filling the air, hearts open wide.
Glistening white upon the ground,
In this magic, love is found.

Children laugh, their joy displayed,
Creating paths where memories played.
Every flake a story told,
In the beauty of winter's fold.

Wish upon the frosty night,
Dreams awaken in delight.
Under moon's soft, tender light,
We celebrate the season bright.

Together we share this dance,
In nature's arms, we take a chance.
Hearts entwined, spirits free,
In this festive tapestry.

Frost-Kissed Whispers

Frost-kissed whispers fill the air,
Gentle secrets, treasures rare.
With every breath, the magic swells,
In the tales that winter tells.

Laughter echoes in the night,
Under stars, a wondrous sight.
Gathered round, we find our place,
In the warmth of friendship's grace.

Pine trees draped in silver sheen,
A festive glow, soft and keen.
From frosty branches, dreams descend,
In this moment, hearts will mend.

Together we savor the cheer,
With joyful voices loud and clear.
As the season wraps us tight,
We're woven in this glowing light.

The Lattice of Frosted Dreams

In the glow of twinkling lights,
Children laugh and dance with glee,
Whispers of joy fill the night's air,
A tapestry woven, wild and free.

Snowflakes flutter down from above,
Each one a story, each one a wish,
Under the stars, in frost we trust,
Silent magic, a sweet, tender bliss.

Frosted wishes, dreams collide,
Colors shimmer in the quiet night,
Carols echo softly, hearts entwined,
Embracing warmth, a pure delight.

Laughter lingers as voices blend,
Moments captured, forever near,
In the lattice of frosted dreams,
Joy abounds, the season's cheer.

Celestial Frost and Gentle Glows

In the crisp air, the evening shines,
Celestial frost paints the ground,
Gentle glows from lanterns sway,
Whispers of wonder all around.

Stars above in a velvet sky,
Crystals glimmer on every tree,
Magic twinkles in every eye,
Holiday spirit sets us free.

Warmth from the hearth, stories unfold,
Laughter dances in the chilly breeze,
Heartfelt wishes, treasures untold,
Together we share, moments to seize.

Celestial frost in a timeless tale,
We gather close, near and dear,
Creating memories that shall not pale,
In the glow of love, we persevere.

Evening's Frosted Embrace

As evening falls, the frost descends,
An embrace of chill that feels so right,
Candles flicker, warmth extends,
Families gather, hearts ignite.

The world is wrapped in a silver hue,
Joyous laughter fills the air,
Spirits soaring, old and new,
In this moment, worry I spare.

Snowflakes dance like a playful tune,
Each one unique, they spin and twirl,
Under the watch of the bright full moon,
Magic lingers, a joyous swirl.

With every smile, we embrace the night,
In frost's soft arms, we find our way,
Evening whispers, holding us tight,
In festive spirit, we choose to stay.

Shards of Light in the Frost

Shards of light break through the frost,
Illuminating joy in every heart,
Frosted windows, warmth embossed,
Together we craft the finest art.

In the stillness, laughter rings,
Voices knit in patterns bright,
Dancing shadows, as our joy sings,
Creating memories in the soft twilight.

Each flickering flame tells a story,
A renewal of hope, a festive cheer,
Wrapped in peace, a glow of glory,
In the chill of night, we hold what's dear.

Let the shards of light glow evermore,
As we gather close, hand in hand,
In the embrace of frost, we explore,
A celebration of life, warm and grand.

The Stillness Beneath the Stars

Beneath the stars, we gather near,
Laughter and joy fill the crisp night air.
Candles flicker, casting soft light,
Hearts unite in this festive sight.

Friends and family, smiles aglow,
A tapestry woven from love's warm flow.
Stories retold, and memories shared,
In this stillness, we know we cared.

The night sky twinkles, a grand display,
As we dance in the shadows, in merry array.
The music soars, lifting our spirits high,
Under the vast, starry, joyous sky.

And as the moments drift like the breeze,
We hold onto laughter with grace and ease.
In the stillness beneath where dreams take flight,
Our hearts sing together, pure delight.

Whispering Pines in the Moonlight

In the whispering pines, the moonlight glows,
Gentle rustlings where the cool wind blows.
Laughter echoes through shadows deep,
As nature cradles us in her sweep.

Fireflies dance in a glimmering row,
Illuminating paths where delight will flow.
Candles flicker, casting soft, warm light,
Embracing the magic of this sweet night.

Voices rise in a festive cheer,
As the heart of the moment draws us near.
Beneath the moon's watch, we share and sing,
In the arms of the woods, our spirits take wing.

The laughter lingers like the summer breeze,
In the whispering pines, our souls find ease.
Together we bask in the joy we create,
As the night unfolds, we celebrate fate.

A Symphony of Frost

In the early dawn, a sparkle bright,
The world adorned in frosty white light.
Each tree and twig, a crystal-bound dream,
Nature whispers in this magical theme.

Children's laughter fills the sparkling air,
Building snowmen without a care.
Snowflakes dance as we frolic about,
In a symphony of frost, without a doubt.

The sun climbs high, casting shadows long,
While we spin and twirl to a winter's song.
A cozy fire awaits with warmth inside,
And tales of wonder are shared with pride.

As evening falls, the stars peek through,
We marvel at all the wondrous view.
In this frosty realm, our hearts are free,
Creating memories, a heartfelt jubilee.

Light Upon the Snow-Covered Landscape

Light upon the snow creates a glow,
Transforming the earth in a quiet show.
Blankets of white spread far and wide,
As whispers of winter our hearts abide.

Footsteps crunch in a rhythmic dance,
Nature invites us, prompting a chance.
With every step, new paths we make,
In this snowy canvas, we boldly partake.

Children's gleeful shouts fill the air,
As they tumble and roll without a care.
A vision of joy, wrapped in winter's embrace,
In this serene beauty, we find our place.

As twilight descends, the stars begin to shine,
We gather together, sharing wishes divine.
Light upon the snow, our spirits entwined,
In love and in laughter, our hearts aligned.

The Echo of Soft Footfalls in the Snow

Whispers of laughter dance in the air,
As snowflakes twirl with a playful flair.
Footfalls crunch in a soft, white coat,
A trail of joy on which we float.

The streetlamps glow, casting warm light,
While children build dreams in the night.
Sleds glide by with a joyful cheer,
In this winter wonderland, we hold dear.

Snowmen stand proud, with scarves held high,
Under the stars in the vast, dark sky.
Hot cocoa comforts, sweet and warm,
In the heart of winter, we feel the charm.

Together we sing, our spirits soar,
Echoing laughter forevermore.
With each soft step, we weave delight,
In the magic of every wintry night.

A Tapestry of White Beneath the Glistening Sky

A blanket of white, so pure and bright,
Covers the ground, a beautiful sight.
Children's voices fill the crisp air,
Creating a tapestry beyond compare.

Snowflakes shimmer as they fall down,
Turning the world into a sparkling crown.
Laughter erupts from every street,
As friends reconnect and share a treat.

Holiday lights twinkle, colors blend,
Signaling joy that will never end.
Gathered around fires, stories abound,
In this festivity, love can be found.

Under the glistening sky up high,
We cherish moments as time goes by.
Hand in hand, spirits rise and gleam,
In the magic of winter, we dream our dream.

Dusk's Embrace in a Quiet Village

As dusk falls softly on the quiet street,
Families gather, their hearts skip a beat.
Windows aglow, flickering lights,
A warmth spreads wide on this chilly night.

The village hums with a festive cheer,
Voices of loved ones, sweet and clear.
Shared laughter echoes, breaking the calm,
Each moment together, a soothing balm.

Snow gently falls, a soft serenade,
Painting the rooftops in frosted jade.
With carols sung beneath the stars,
We toast to friendship and love from afar.

In this embrace, a memory made,
As hearts unite, not one will fade.
Through the laughter, a treasure we find,
In dusk's gentle hold, our souls intertwined.

The Secret Language of Feathered Snowflakes

Snowflakes dance down with a secret grace,
Whirling and twirling, a soft, white lace.
Each one unique, a story to tell,
In the hush of winter, all is well.

They whisper softly as they touch the ground,
Painting the world in a silence profound.
Children listen with gleaming eyes,
To the magic in the winter skies.

Playful debates of who can catch,
The prettiest flake, a gentle match.
Frosty breath mingles in the chill,
As moments unfold, time stands still.

In this quiet language, hearts collide,
With laughter and joy as our joyful guide.
We savor the whispers that float all around,
In the secret of snowflakes, love is found.

The Softness of Snow's Touch

In whispers of white, the snowflakes fall,
Each flake a promise, a soft, sweet call.
Laughter in the air, joy's gentle swirl,
A blanket of winter, as dreams unfurl.

Children bundled tight, they dance all around,
In this winter wonder, bliss can be found.
Snowmen stand proudly, with smiles so wide,
A magical world, where hearts open wide.

Evening brings warmth, with fires aglow,
Dancing sparks fly, as embers throw.
Families gather close, sharing their cheer,
Tales of the snow, as the end of year nears.

Under the starlit sky, the moon's gentle glow,
A scene painted softly, in winter's show.
Feel the softness of snow, pure and bright,
In its tender embrace, we find our delight.

Pristine Quietude at Dusk

The sun dips low, painting skies of gold,
A canvas of dreams, whispering untold.
Trees stand tall, draped in twilight's grace,
Each shadow a secret, each moment we chase.

The silence wraps round like a warm embrace,
Nature holds her breath in this sacred space.
Stars peek through, blink as the night draws near,
A tapestry woven, of hope and cheer.

Crickets chirp softly, a lullaby sweet,
As the world slows down, and hearts skip a beat.
In this stillness, laughter echoes through,
Gathered under the sky, friends old and new.

Candles flicker bright, casting warm light,
Reflections of joy in this beautiful sight.
The evening unfolds with a gentle sigh,
Pristine quietude, where spirits can fly.

Light Prancing on Icy Trails

Morning light glimmers on paths paved with ice,
A sparkling wonder, a treasure so nice.
Laughter and joy echo through the air,
As skaters glide gracefully, free without care.

Children in sleds race down hills with cheer,
Shouting with joy as they conquer their fear.
The chill in the air, but hearts beat so warm,
As friendships are forged in this magical storm.

Hot cocoa awaits, in mugs filled with love,
Steam rises softly, as if sent from above.
The warmth of togetherness, brightened the day,
Spreading smiles and laughter along the way.

As sunlight fades, dance beneath the stars,
The glow of the moon, like shimmering scars.
Ice trails pave the way for memories made,
A tapestry woven, as friendships cascade.

Serenity Wrapped in White

Blankets of white wrap the world in calm,
The hush of the night, like a soothing balm.
Underneath stars, the earth takes a sigh,
As beauty unfolds beneath the night sky.

Frost-kissed branches, cradling dreams,
Nature sings softly, in delicate streams.
A moment of peace, where time stands still,
Whispers of winter, a heart left to fill.

Gather 'round fires, let stories be told,
In the warmth of each other, watch magic unfold.
Laughter and love, they twirl in the air,
Serenity wrapped in moments we share.

As snowflakes fall gently, a dance to behold,
A canvas of white, with wonders untold.
In the stillness of night, all seems so right,
Wrapped in serenity, our hearts become light.

The Calm After the Storm

The skies are clear, the sun peeks through,
Colors dance, in a brilliant hue.
Whispers of joy spread all around,
Peaceful laughter is the joyful sound.

Puddles gleam where raindrops stay,
Children gather to jump and play.
Nature's smile, fresh and bright,
A world reborn, a pure delight.

Flowers blossom, colors on display,
The fragrance sweetens the vibrant day.
Friendship blooms in a sunny embrace,
Together, we cherish this sacred space.

So let us dance under the sky,
With hearts so light, we're free to fly.
The calm now rests, the storm has passed,
In this moment, joy holds fast.

Celestial Hues of Dusk

The sun dips low, painting the skies,
With strokes of orange, where beauty lies.
Stars begin to twinkle bright,
As night unfolds, embracing light.

Crisp air carries a joyful song,
As laughter echoes all night long.
Families gather, sharing cheer,
In this serene moment, love draws near.

Candle flames flicker, shadows play,
Illuminating memories of the day.
Soft whispers linger, hearts entwine,
In celestial hues, our spirits shine.

Each twilight brings a gift anew,
A canvas painted in fading blue.
Together we bask in the glowing dusk,
In this moment, life's sweet husk.

Crystalline Dreams Awaken

Morning breaks with a silvery gleam,
Awakening hearts with a radiant beam.
Crystalline snowflakes fall with grace,
Wrapping the world in a soft embrace.

Children's laughter fills the air,
Building snowmen with joy and care.
Sleds racing down the hills so steep,
In this winter wonder, memories we keep.

Hot cocoa warms our hands so tight,
As we gather round, with faces bright.
Stories shared by the crackling fire,
In crystalline dreams, we never tire.

The sun sets low, painting the snow,
A sparkling canvas, a wondrous glow.
Together we cherish this frosted land,
In dreams awakened, hand in hand.

Luminous Shadows on Snow

The moonlight dances on snow so white,
Casting shadows in the still of night.
Whispers soft of the winter breeze,
In this moment, the world's at ease.

Footsteps crunch on frosted ground,
Where magic lingers all around.
Hushed voices share secrets low,
In the glow of night, our spirits grow.

Stars are twinkling, bright as fire,
In this serene, wintry choir.
With every heartbeat, joy we sow,
As luminous shadows on the snow.

Together wrapped in a blanket warm,
Feeling the peace, a soothing charm.
In the quiet night, we find our way,
In luminous shadows, forever stay.

Frosted Pines Under a Silver Moon

The frosted pines stand tall and proud,
Beneath the moon's soft silver shroud.
Whispers of joy dance on the breeze,
As stars twinkle with such gentle ease.

Laughter echoes, hearts so light,
In the glow of this magical night.
Fires crackle, warming the air,
While dreams take flight without a care.

Snowflakes twirl, a joyful sight,
Each one unique, pure delight.
Gathered friends share stories bright,
In this festive, wintry light.

The world awaits, wrapped in white,
Bathed in love, shining so bright.
Frosted pines whisper and sway,
Embracing the joy of this winter's day.

In the Embrace of Icicle Shadows

Icicles glisten, a sparkling show,
Hanging down from roofs below.
Crisp air fills the joyous night,
With shadows dancing in soft light.

Children laugh, their cheeks aglow,
As winter's magic starts to flow.
Sleds slide down the hill with glee,
In this wonderland, wild and free.

The bonfire crackles, sparks take flight,
Under the canopy of starry night.
Songs of joy ring clear and loud,
As we gather with love, so proud.

In every flake that falls from skies,
In every cheer and bright surprise,
The embrace of winter wraps us whole,
Filling each heart, warming the soul.

Serenity Wrapped in a White Blanket

A blanket of snow covers the earth,
Whispers of peace, a moment of mirth.
Footprints echo through the serene,
In this wonderland, so pristine.

Fires glow with a golden hue,
As families gather, old and new.
Stories shared with each passing hour,
Bonds grow stronger, love a flower.

The aroma of cookies fills the air,
Laughter sparkles everywhere.
Wrapped in coziness, warm and bright,
We revel in this joyous night.

Serenity reigns, a gentle embrace,
Life feels lighter in this space.
Together we celebrate, hearts aglow,
In the beauty of winter's snowy show.

Shimmering Tranquility of Frozen Streams

Frozen streams shimmer under the light,
Reflecting twinkles, a magical sight.
Footsteps crunch on the icy path,
Nature's chorus sings joy's aftermath.

Snowflakes dance upon the air,
Twinkling laughter, beauty rare.
In this tranquil winter's spell,
Stories of joy and peace we tell.

The sky blushes in twilight's grace,
As stars appear, taking their place.
Frost-kissed branches gently sway,
Inviting dreams to play and stay.

Through this wonder, hearts unite,
In whispers of magic, pure delight.
Shimmering streams, under the moon,
Filling our souls with a festive tune.

The Quietude of Frost-Kissed Forests

Whispers of snow, a soft laughter,
Glittering branches, dance ever after.
Footprints abound in the crisp, white ground,
Magic in silence, the joy is profound.

Icicles hang like delicate gems,
Painting the trees in bright, frozen hems.
Laughter of children, the chill in their breath,
Echoes of wonder, a life full of zest.

Beneath the frost, the earth takes a sigh,
Under this blanket, the dreams softly lie.
Nature adorned in her wintery grace,
A festive allure, a warm, cozy space.

As stars twinkle bright, the night takes a hold,
The forest a secret, a story retold.
Join hands with loved ones, let the warmth abide,
In the quietude, let our spirits glide.

Light Through the Frosty Veil

Sunrise bursts forth in a splash of gold,
Lighting the crystals, a sight to behold.
Frosty veil lifting, the world comes alive,
Joyous celebrations, together we thrive.

Candles are glowing, their flickers like dreams,
Mirroring laughter, wrapping us in beams.
Old stories are shared, in the chill of the air,
Each moment a treasure, each heart lays it bare.

Songs fill the breeze, with notes pure and clear,
Voices entwined, as we dance without fear.
With each twirl and spin, we twinkle like stars,
In the warmth of the light, forgetting our scars.

Evening sets in, with a hush so profound,
Twinkling lights echo the love we have found.
Gathered together, a bond we can't sever,
In this frosty embrace, we are light, we are forever.

A Palette of Gentle Chill

Brushstrokes of blue on the horizon's face,
Glistening snowflakes, nature's soft lace.
Fires roaring bright, casting shadows and cheer,
Gathering together, with loved ones so dear.

Savor the warmth of the cocoa's embrace,
Gifts wrapped with laughter, each smile holds a place.
Charming the cold with our stories untold,
In this festive spirit, as memories unfold.

The world may be frosted, but hearts glow with light,
Adventures await under blanket of white.
Cheerful connections, as laughter takes flight,
In the palette of winter, we find pure delight.

Beneath the clear sky, where the stars doth play,
Each moment a canvas, we weave night and day.
Together we wander through joy and goodwill,
With colors of kindness, we dance in the chill.

Twilight's Shimmering Canvas

As twilight descends, paints a world anew,
With strokes of lavender and whispers of blue.
Heaven above, with its glistening light,
Gathers us close in the soft winter night.

Shadows grow long, but our laughter stays bright,
A tapestry woven in warm hues of white.
Stories erupt like the crackling of fire,
Instilling in moments a spark of desire.

Tinsel and ribbons adorn every bough,
Joy fills the air, there's a magic right now.
Sparkling eyes glimmer as ember flame glows,
Festive reflections in soft drifts of snow.

With family around and hot cider in hand,
We toast to the moments we take on demand.
In twilight's embrace, we'll cherish the thrill,
Creating a canvas, our hearts ever still.

Frost's Gentle Artistry

A whispering chill in the air,
Magic dances, everywhere.
Icicles drip with a twinkling light,
Nature's canvas, pure delight.

Children laugh, their breath like steam,
Building castles, living the dream.
Snowflakes twirl in a playful waltz,
Frost's gentle touch, without faults.

Hot cocoa steams in mugs held tight,
Fires crackle, spreading warm light.
Joyful spirits gather near,
Celebrating this time of year.

The world transformed, a glittering gem,
Under the moon's soft, silver hem.
Frost's gentle artistry shines bright,
A festive spectacle, pure delight.

The Beauty of Stillness

The world hushed beneath a snow-white quilt,
In every corner, magic is built.
Stars twinkle softly, a distant cheer,
In this beauty, there's nothing to fear.

Candles flicker in frosted glass,
Whispers of peace as moments pass.
Silent nights that seem to glow,
Wrapped in warmth, a gentle flow.

The quiet streets, a sparkling maze,
Drifting in dreams, we stand amazed.
Snowflakes fall with a delicate grace,
Every moment is a sweet embrace.

Nature smiles in its tranquil pose,
In stillness, the heart finds repose.
The beauty of now, forever adored,
In this peaceful season, we're restored.

Twilight's Cool Caress

As day fades out, the twilight gleams,
Colors merge, like painted dreams.
The evening calls with a silken sigh,
Magic blooms as the stars light the sky.

Frosty whispers, a tender touch,
Under the glow, we gather as such.
Laughter flows like a gentle stream,
In twilight's embrace, we weave our dream.

The air is crisp, the world aglow,
Each ember sparks a festive show.
With loved ones close, we share delight,
Under the spell of the soft twilight.

As night unfolds with a twinkling grace,
We find our hearts in this wondrous place.
Twilight's cool caress, a cherished song,
In this festive hour, we all belong.

Enchanted Nights in the Snow

The moon glistens on a blanket wide,
In enchanted nights, we take pride.
Whispers of dreams float on the breeze,
In the joy of winter, hearts find ease.

Snowflakes flutter like delicate lace,
Painting the world in a gentle embrace.
Laughter and stories fill the air,
Enchanted nights, beyond compare.

The crackle of wood, the warmth of fire,
Bringing us closer, kindling desire.
With every twinkle, hope ignites,
In the magic of these snowy nights.

Gathered together, our spirits soar,
In this festive moment, we want more.
Enchanted nights, with hearts aglow,
In the beauty of winter's soft show.